Ferdinand Magellan

◆◆◆◆◆◆◆◆◆◆◆◆◆◆

Ferdinand Magellan

BY
JON NOONAN

ILLUSTRATED BY YOSHI MIYAKE

CRESTWOOD HOUSE
NEW YORK

Maxwell Macmillan Canada
Toronto

Maxwell Macmillan International
New York Oxford Singapore Sydney

To my relatives,
past, present and future.

CRESTWOOD HOUSE
Macmillan Publishing Company
866 Third Avenue, New York, NY 10022

Maxwell Macmillan Canada, Inc.
1200 Eglinton Avenue East, Suite 200
Don Mills, Ontario M3C 3N1

Macmillan Publishing Company is part of the
Maxwell Communication Group of Companies

First Edition
Book design by Sylvia Frezzolini
Printed in the United States of America

10 9 8 7 6 5 4 3 2 1

LIBRARY OF CONGRESS CATALOGING-IN-PUBLICATION DATA
Noonan, Jon.
Ferdinand Magellan / Jon Noonan.
p.   cm. — (Explorers)
Includes Index.
Summary: Presents the life story of the Portuguese sea captain who commanded the first expedition to sail around the world.
ISBN 0-89686-706-4
1. Magalhães, Fernao de, d. 1521. 2. Explorers—Portugal—Biography—Juvenile literature.   3. Voyages around the world—Juvenile literature.   [1. Magellan, Ferdinand, d. 1521. 2. Explorers. 3. Voyages around the world.]   I. Title. II. Series: Noonan, Jon. Explorers.
G286.M2A6   1993   91–38219
910.92—dc20
[B]

CONTENTS

THE ADVENTURES OF
MAGELLAN AND SERRANO   7
   Mission for Magellan
   Magellan Saves His Cousin
   Pirates!

YOUNG FERDINAND MAGELLAN   17
   Magellan as a Boy
   Christopher Columbus's Visit
   Court of the New King

MAGELLAN GETS TO GO   21
   The Sailing Ships
   Unfriendly Greeting
   Magellan's First Conflict
   On to India
   Lands to the East

MAGELLAN LOSES HIS COMMAND   27
   Spain

CAPTAIN GENERAL MAGELLAN   31
   Captain Cartagena
   South America
   Mutiny!
   The Strait Is Found
   The Pacific Ocean
   Guam
   The Philippines
   Magellan on Mactan
   Home from the Spice Islands

MAGELLAN'S EFFORTS INSPIRE OTHERS   46

GLOSSARY   47
INDEX   48

THE ADVENTURES OF MAGELLAN AND SERRANO

Early in his life, Ferdinand Magellan became known for his great courage. One of the first times Magellan displayed courage occurred in September 1509.

Floating in a city harbor on the coast of Malaysia, five sailing ships from Portugal could be seen. Standing on the fourth ship, Ferdinand Magellan and Francisco Serrano gazed at the city called Malacca. These young men lived as common sailors. In the future, they would become captains of their own ships.

Ferdinand and Francisco were cousins. They wished to earn fame and fortune by sailing to the important trading centers of Asia. Malacca was the largest and richest city they had ever seen.

The captain general (Captain Sequeira) and some of his officers were in the city visiting its ruler. When they came back to the ships, the captain general gave shore leave to the crew. The city's ruler said the Portuguese sailors could feel free to trade and walk about Malacca.

It seemed too good to be true. The ruler of the city had given gifts to the captain general and his officers. He gave them a great feast at his palace that stood high above Malacca. He treated them like friends of his family—yet they had first landed at this city just one day ago.

Each of the five ships had its own captain. The captain of Magellan's ship, Captain Sousa, was not sure the city's leader could be trusted. He sent Magellan and Serrano to try to find out if the ruler had other plans.

Magellan and Serrano saw people from many countries trading in the crowded city. At that time, Malacca was one of the largest trading centers in the world.

Traders from Ceylon (a large island south of India now called Sri Lanka) brought diamonds, pearls, rubies, sapphires and other gems. Chinese traders came with silk, brass and finely crafted sculptures. Traders from India displayed cloths of **cashmere** and **calico.** Arab traders sold special

spices such as cinnamon, ginger, cloves, pepper and nutmeg.

Serrano learned from a Chinese woman that the city's ruler was only pretending to be a friend of the sailors from Portugal. The ruler had been told by other traders that the sailors were coming to his city. He hoped to take the Portuguese ships for himself while their crews traded on the shore. In these times there were few international laws and stealing between nations was common.

Serrano reported his findings to Captain Sousa. Sousa tried to warn the captain general. The captain general still wanted to believe that Malacca's leader was his friend. The ruler was having a great many sacks of precious pepper stacked on the shore for the sailors to take as gifts. The gem traders also said they had a new supply of gems to sell for a special low price. Almost all the Portuguese officers and crew eagerly left their ships for the shore.

Captain Sousa sent Serrano and some of his crew to the docks to guard the sailors. Magellan stayed on their ship as a lookout. He saw several boats loaded with Malay men coming toward their ships. Magellan saw that they all carried knives. He warned his captain.

Mission for Magellan

This time, Captain Sousa sent Magellan to see the captain general. Magellan got into the one small boat that had not been taken to the shore. He rowed swiftly to the captain general's ship and saw that he was playing a game of chess.

Many Malays surrounded him. They acted as though they liked to watch the captain general play the game. They were actually waiting for a signal of smoke from the city ruler's palace. At the signal, they would start their attack.

Magellan knew the Malays could not speak his language. In a calm voice, he told the captain general that they were in danger. The Malays all had knives close at hand. They were getting ready to take over the Portuguese ships.

The captain general ordered his crew leader to gather the crew. He calmly continued his chess game. Then he saw one of the Malays take out a sharp knife! The captain general jumped up and stabbed him with his dagger. Some of the crew cleared the other Malays from the ship. They fired the cannon into the Malay boats around them.

Great numbers of Malays were on the shore. They attacked the sailors as they raced to their small boats. Serrano and his fellow crew members tried to guard them. There were too many Malays. Several sailors were being caught and killed.

Magellan Saves His Cousin

Magellan saw his cousin fighting bravely on the dock. He leaped into his boat and rowed toward Serrano with two other sailors. They saved Serrano and several others and returned to Captain Sousa's ship. The five Portuguese ships gathered the survivors and set sail for safer waters.

In the open sea, Captain Sousa's ship was the slowest of the five. It had been built to carry horses. Although the horses had been left on the shore, the ship was not as easy to steer as the others.

The other ships were in a hurry. Sousa's ship was left behind.

Pirates!

But not for long. A four-masted Chinese pirate ship saw them. It came upon them swiftly and **grappled** to their side. The Chinese swarmed onto Sousa's ship. The Portuguese wore strong armor and stepped into the **fray** with their swords. They sliced the pirates until the survivors fled back to their ship. The pirates cut the ropes that held them to Sousa's ship and tried to sail away.

Serrano and a small group of Sousa's crewmen were still on the Chinese ship. The Chinese surrounded them. Since Sousa's ship was so hard to steer, Magellan and four others threw the small boat overboard. It was the same boat Magellan had used to save Serrano at Malacca. The five sailors quickly rowed across the gap to the back end (the stern) of the pirate ship.

Magellan and his crew slashed the pirates at one end while Serrano and his crew slashed from the other end. The few pirates left threw down their weapons and surrendered.

Magellan was short in height but strong in spirit. He had saved Serrano again.

The Chinese ship was in better shape than Sousa's. Captain Sousa and the crew took it over and left their slow ship behind. The pirate ship was so fast that it caught up with the other Portuguese ships in two days.

For their courage and leadership, Magellan and Serrano were soon called captains. They were each put in command of their own ship.

Serrano used his ship to sail for the Spice Islands to the east of Malaysia. He wrote letters to Magellan asking him to come there too. Magellan wrote back and said he would try to make the trip. If Portugal would not let him go there by sailing east, then he said he would go there "by the way of Spain," sailing west like the Spanish ships that sailed to the new lands of America.

By sailing in the Spanish direction and crossing the islands around Malaysia again, Magellan could be the first person to sail around the world.

He simply wanted to see the Spice Islands, visit the lands nearby and see his cousin again. One day, Magellan would command a fleet of Spanish ships that would voyage west across the uncharted Pacific Ocean to the Spice Islands. One of the ships would sail all the way around the world to return to Spain. It took a brave captain, Captain Ferdinand Magellan, to get the trip started.

YOUNG FERDINAND MAGELLAN

Magellan as a Boy

In about the year 1480, Ferdinand Magellan was born in a town in northern Portugal. In his native language, his full given name was Fernão de Magalhães. He lived with his older brother, Diogo, and his older sister Isabel. Ferdinand's parents died when he was about 10 years old. Several towns today claim to be his birthplace. He is thought to have spent his early youth in Ponte da Barca and Sabrosa.

At about age 12 Ferdinand was sent by his family to live at the court of the queen of Portugal, Queen Leonora. She was the queen to King John II. Only children of certain families friendly to the king and queen were granted this honor.

Ferdinand's cousin Francisco Serrano, also 12, came to the court at the same time. Magellan's 14-year-old brother, Diogo, had started there two years earlier. Along with other boys, they were given lessons in how to steer ships by the stars, read maps and charts, ride horses, hunt and fight with skill using a sword or **lance** in either hand. The queen's 22-year-old brother, Duke Manuel, was in charge of some of their studies. In the future he would become the new king.

The boys also worked as **pages.** They had to deliver messages, clean rooms and do other chores.

Christopher Columbus's Visit

In March 1493 Columbus landed on the coast of Portugal on his return from his first voyage to America. He visited with King John II before going on to Spain. Columbus thought he had found a way to China and India by sailing west around the world. He brought West Indies natives back with him. Because he thought the islands he found were close to India, he called the people Indians.

The boys at the court were excited by his news. Some of them likely dreamed of growing up to be an explorer like Columbus someday.

Later Magellan learned that Columbus had not sailed around the world. The lands Columbus found were not close to India or China. Magellan grew up with the dream of completing what Columbus had set out to do.

Court of the New King

In 1495 King John II died. His brother-in-law Duke Manuel became the new king.

Magellan soon started working at King Manuel's court. He had been raised in rank from a page to a **squire.** Instead of household chores he kept records of the king's sailing ship supplies.

In 1497, the 28-year-old explorer Vasco da Gama left Portugal with a fleet of four ships to seek India by sailing east. Although young Magellan wished to go too, he had to stay at the king's court. Da Gama came back two years later. He spoke of his success in finding India after sailing around Africa. Although only two of his ships survived the trip his cargo of spices was still worth more than the cost of the entire voyage.

Captain Pedro Cabral was given command of 13 ships for the second voyage to India. He and his fleet left Portugal in 1500. About half of his ships survived the stormy voyage. These ships came back loaded with gems, fine cloths, spices and crafted works of art.

MAGELLAN GETS TO GO

Magellan longed to see the cities of India for himself. In 1505 his turn finally came. Captain general Almeida was given command of a 22-ship fleet to set up naval bases along the way to India. Magellan, as well as his brother and cousin, got to go with the captain general.

The Sailing Ships

Most of these sailing ships had three masts. Each mast was a strong, tall pole of wood used to carry the ship's sails. The first two masts carried large square sails. The third pole carried a triangular-shaped sail. Each mast had a walled platform of wood built near its top. Reaching the platforms by rope ladders, the sailors used them for lookouts and high places to shoot arrows at their enemies.

The largest of these ships could carry about 100 tons of cargo. If some of them survived the voyage, they could carry enough gold, special spices and gems to make the king happy.

Unfriendly Greeting

The fleet sailed through the Atlantic Ocean and rounded the southern tip of Africa at the stormy Cape of Good Hope. The captain general then set up his first naval base at Kilwa in the summer of 1505. This coastal city (in the country called Tanzania today) was almost halfway up the Indian Ocean side of Africa.

The Kilwa's leader was a Persian called Ibrahim. (Persia is called Iran today.) He had been visited on the second voyage of Vasco da Gama three years earlier. Ibrahim agreed to always be friendly to sailors from Portugal. He also said he would give some gold for their king each year they visited his city. In the following years, Ibrahim had not kept to his agreement with Vasco do Gama.

The captain general was ordered by the king to see if Ibrahim had changed for the better. If not, an Arab leader known to be friendly to the Portuguese king was to be put in his place by force. At this time Arabs still controlled much of the trade between Africa, India, China, Malaysia and the Spice Islands.

Ibrahim did not welcome the captain general's ships when they arrived. The captain general sent one of his officers into the city to set up meetings with him.

Twice the city leader agreed to meet the captain general. Both times he did not come. The captain general saw that Ibrahim was treating him poorly. He chose to take action to get the city leader's attention. Perhaps by this example the leaders of other trading centers would choose to be more friendly.

Magellan's First Conflict

The captain general sent 500 sailors to take over the city of 12,000 people. Since Magellan, as well as his brother and cousin, had suits of armor, they were allowed to go too. This battle was their first chance to make full use of the weapons training they had gained at the king's school.

The sailors landed on the shore and climbed over the city walls. Step by step they fought the city's soldiers on their way to Ibrahim's palace. The arrows and spears of the soldiers had little effect on the sailors' strong armor. The sailors fought with swords, shields, lances and **crossbows.**

Ferdinand Magellan and his two comrades lived through the fight. The city was soon won and

Ibrahim fled. The Arab leader Mohammed was put in his place.

On to India

The sailors guarded the trading centers on the east coast of Africa for two years. In 1507 Magellan's brother sailed home to Portugal. Magellan and his cousin continued on to India.

By early 1509 the Portuguese had control of several trading centers on the coast of India too. Arab traders did not like newcomers taking over their trade. In February the sailors won a sea battle against the Arabs in the harbor of Diu at the tip of India's west coast. Magellan helped capture an Egyptian flagship but he was severely wounded. He recovered at Cochin on the southwest Indian coast.

Soon Portugal was trying to control the eastern Indian Ocean as well. That summer Magellan sailed to Malacca, Malaysia. Then after some time in India, Magellan served in the waters of Malaysia again for almost two years.

Lands to the East

After Serrano and Magellan became captains they each took their ships on a side trip to the east. Serrano landed at the Spice Islands. These islands are above Australia, which was then an uncharted land.

Magellan voyaged across the South China Sea to seek lands east of the Spice Islands. He sailed about 2,000 miles. On the way stood the islands of the Philippines. After Magellan returned to Portugal, he reported that he wanted goods to trade at the islands he found.

MAGELLAN LOSES HIS COMMAND

But Magellan had not been given orders to go so far to the east. He had chosen to explore on his own without permission. His command of the ship was taken away and he was sent home.

In 1513 Magellan returned to work at the king's court. He hoped he would be given a high title and pay for his good services. Instead he was given a lowly title not much better than the squire position he had held as a boy. Magellan was shocked that all his years of brave action amounted to little in the eyes of the king's court. For a long time Magellan tried to improve his standing.

He went to fight in Morocco, south of Portugal, where his commander gave him a high title for his efforts. Others were filled with envy at Magellan's success. After the commander died they wrote letters to the king, speaking poorly of Magellan. Magellan returned to Portugal again. This time he came back with a lame leg. In a Moroccan battle his knee was hurt by a lance.

Magellan tried to get the attention of his king. He wrote a letter telling of his loyal service and asked to see him. Magellan hoped to get permission for a special voyage to the Spice Islands and the lands he had seen beyond the South China Sea.

When Magellan saw him, King Manuel said no to all of his requests. He added that he saw no need for Magellan in his kingdom.

Spain

Magellan was no longer welcome in his homeland. In 1517 he left his country.

After coming to the city of Seville Magellan started a new life in Spain. He soon became engaged to be married to Beatriz, the Spanish cousin of one of his friends, Duarte Barbosa. Within weeks they were married.

Magellan's goal was still to command a ship to the Spice Islands. Beatriz's father, Diogo Barbosa, tried to help him. They hoped to get approval for the trip from King Charles, the new king of

Spain. After efforts through several Spanish leaders, Magellan got to see him.

King Charles was 17 years old. He was impressed with Magellan and awed by the stories of his ocean voyages. He said yes to Magellan's plans. He signed a contract for the Spice Island voyage in March 1518. Magellan was happy. The king chose him to be the captain general.

CAPTAIN GENERAL MAGELLAN

Five Spanish ships were put under Magellan's command—the *Trinidad, San Antonio, Victoria, Concepcion* and *Santiago*. They were in need of repair so Magellan and his crew spent several months getting them ready.

Many items for trade were loaded on the ships, including knives, colorful cloths, bells, fishhooks, mirrors and bracelets. The food included biscuits, nuts, salted meat, figs, raisins and great numbers of **casks** of fresh water.

Magellan's captains and other officers were Spanish along with a few Portuguese. The crews came from Spain, Portugal, Italy and France as well as some from Germany, Greece, Africa and one from England.

They set sail from Spain in September 1519. Magellan's first stop was at the Spanish Canary Islands. He landed there to pick up extra supplies.

While there Magellan was met by a fast sailboat sent from Spain by Diogo Barbosa. The boat's leader warned Magellan that Barbosa had heard the Spanish captains were going to try to take over command of the voyage soon. If Magellan did not go along with them, they planned to kill him.

Magellan was not worried. Most of the officers were the spoiled sons of wealthy Spanish leaders. They loaded their ships with servants to take care of them. One of them, Captain Cartagena, brought ten servants just for himself. Magellan thought he could keep these easy-living officers under control.

Magellan ordered the Spanish captains to follow him. He took the ships around the windy western bulge of Africa.

Then he set a course for the southern coast of Brazil. Its northern coast was already claimed by Portugal and was off-limits to Spanish ships.

Captain Cartagena

Captain Cartagena wanted to be the captain general. During the cross-Atlantic voyage Cartagena chose not to salute Magellan. Magellan called all the captains to his cabin. In the steady wind they were able to bring their ships up to Magellan's so they could board his ship.

In his cabin Captain Cartagena tried to make Magellan angry. He wanted an excuse to kill Magellan. No matter what Cartagena said Magellan stayed calm. Then Cartagena became angry.

In front of all the captains he said he would not obey Magellan anymore. Magellan signaled his sailors and they rushed into his cabin with their weapons ready. Cartagena blurted out that he and the other Spanish captains were planning to kill Magellan. Such statements were acts of mutiny so Cartagena was made a prisoner.

Magellan continued the voyage. After Brazil was sighted Magellan sailed to the south until they were far from Portuguese ships.

South America

They first landed at a village where the city of Rio de Janeiro is today. Magellan called it Santa Lucia. The natives were friendly and much trading took place.

After two weeks, they set sail again and landed at the Rio de la Plata, between today's Uruguay and Argentina. Magellan hoped this waterway was the pass to the South Sea—the ocean that Vasco Nuñez de Balboa saw from Panama in 1513.

It turned out to be just a river so Magellan headed south again. Some of the officers and crew did not want to go. They were already as far south as the Cape of Good Hope that rounded the bottom of Africa. The weather at sea was getting colder and windier. Maybe there was no pass to the South Sea and they would only freeze and die if they went further.

Magellan was too set in his mind to give up his goal. He led the ships further south through icy storms to a port he named Saint Julian. They did not know it then, but only a few more days of sailing would bring them to the ocean pass they were seeking.

Mutiny!

Once more the Spanish captains tried to cause a mutiny. They freed Cartagena and took over three of the five ships—the *San Antonio*, the *Victoria* and the *Concepcion*. The captain of the *Santiago* stayed loyal to Magellan. He was Francisco Serrano's older brother John.

In the struggle the Spanish captain Quesada stabbed an officer, Juan de Lloriaga, who tried to save the *San Antonio*. Then the captains locked up the others who were still loyal to Magellan. They readied their ships for an attack on Magellan's *Trinidad* and the loyal *Santiago* by its side.

The captain general chose to take strong action. From his ship, the *Trinidad,* Magellan tried to re-take the ships one by one. He sent some sailors to give a message to Captain Mendoza of the *Victoria.* Two of the sailors entered Mendoza's cabin. The message told him to be loyal to Magellan. Mendoza treated it with scorn, so the two sailors thrust their knives into the traitor. The loyal sailors took back the ship and brought it alongside the *Trinidad.*

Then another sailor loyal to Magellan cut the rope to the *San Antonio*'s anchor. The *San Antonio* drifted toward the *Trinidad.* Magellan and his crew boarded the ship and Captain Quesada surrendered too.

Now only the *Concepcion,* captained by Cartagena, was left. Cartagena saw that all was lost. When Magellan's crew came close to him, he surrendered too.

When the ships set sail for the south again, Cartagena was left stranded on the shore with a priest who had sided with him. The loyal officer of the *San Antonio* and Captain Mendoza died of their wounds.

King Charles had granted the captain general the power to kill disloyal officers if necessary, by knife or by hanging. So Captain Quesada, who had killed the loyal *San Antonio* officer, was be-

headed. Magellan let the other Spanish officers live but gave them hard work to do.

Juan Sebastian del Cano was one of these officers. In the future he would be chosen to captain one of Magellan's ships around the world.

The Strait Is Found

Soon the sad crews grew happy again. After some stormy days sailing they found the ocean pass to the South Sea. In a storm, the *Santiago* was shipwrecked but its crew was saved.

Magellan called the pass the Strait of All Saints. Today it is called the Strait of Magellan.

The *San Antonio* was sent to search the southern part of the strait. Once it was away from Magellan, the ship was sailed back to Spain by a Spanish officer. He was too afraid to voyage into the unknown sea.

Magellan still wanted to continue. The *Concepcion* was now captained by John Serrano and the *Victoria* by Duarte Barbosa, the cousin of Magellan's wife. Before leaving the strait the captain general had them load their ships full of fresh fish and birds.

The Pacific Ocean

Then they entered the strange South Sea. Two star **galaxies** were seen in the clear night sky.

Today they are called the Magellanic Clouds.

The sea seemed calm compared to the stormy Atlantic Ocean. Magellan gave the South Sea a new name—the Pacific Ocean (pacific means peaceful).

Magellan and his two friendly captains hoped the Spice Islands would be found a short distance away. Instead they sailed into the largest ocean in the world.

The explorers sailed along the coast of present-day Chile and then headed northwest into the open ocean. Weeks went by without their sighting land.

The ocean seemed endless and empty. The steady wind pushed the ships westward across the **equator.** After almost four months they reached the island of Guam, sighting only two tiny islands along the way.

The sailors suffered greatly from the lack of fresh food and water. Without fruits and vegetables, many of the men died of **scurvy.** The gums of their teeth swelled up so large that some men couldn't eat.

By this time all the food was gone and the water stank. Magellan and his crew were eating sawdust and the leather wrappings off the masts. Guam was a welcome sight.

Guam

Then natives with spears came out in canoes and swarmed onto the Spanish ships. Seeing the sailors so weak, the local people started taking everything they could find.

Some of the sailors scared them with their crossbows and the natives fled. Magellan sent a few dozen men onto the island. They came back loaded with bananas, coconuts, sugarcane, chickens, pigs and casks filled with fresh water. After restocking the ships, Magellan set sail for safer waters.

The Philippines

The Spice Islands stood about 11 **degrees** to the south, close to the equator. Magellan steered north of them to first find the group of islands he had seen before. He found them. The islands of Samar, Limassawa and Cebu were sighted. He had come to the Philippine Islands.

Magellan was the first person to sail completely around the earth. He claimed the islands in the name of King Charles. Magellan knew King Charles would make him governor, the leader of these lands. In this time, it was thought that everyone in the kingdom should share the same religion. So Magellan set about making the king's future subjects Christians.

Magellan on Mactan

One chief on Mactan, an island close to Cebu, and Magellan did not get along. They challenged each other to battle. With less than 50 volunteers Magellan faced more than 1,000 warriors on the Mactan shore.

The chief of Cebu, now a Christian, offered to supply Magellan with 1,000 of his own natives. Magellan said they would not be needed. He had faced overwhelming odds before. If he could win his success could convert all the islands to Christianity.

Luck was not with Magellan that day. He was surrounded by the warriors. He continued to fight while other sailors raced to their boats for safety. With eight other sailors, Magellan was killed. It was April 27, 1521. Eventually the Philippine Islands did become a Christian country.

Home from the Spice Islands

The ships soon left the Philippines. Two of the ships made it to the Spice Islands where they learned that Francisco Serrano had died that year as well.

One ship survived to arrive at Spain loaded with rich spices. It was the *Victoria*. Under the command of Juan Sebastian del Cano, the ship

arrived on September 8, 1522. Less than two dozen sailors came back out of the more than 200 who had started the voyage.

MAGELLAN'S EFFORTS INSPIRE OTHERS

Soon other explorers followed Magellan into the Pacific Ocean. The Spanish conducted trade with the Philippines over two centuries, using **galleons.** English explorers such as Captain James Cook traveled through the Pacific too.

Magellan showed the South Sea to be larger than many could believe. He was the first to sail completely around the earth. Like other great explorers, he opened the minds of others to a wider world.

GLOSSARY

calico—Cotton cloth.

cashmere—Soft wool from the goats of Kashmir and Tibet.

casks—Barrels made of strips of wood.

crossbow—Archery bow on wood stock grooved for shooting arrows.

degrees—Units of measure for arcs and angles, used to find locations on a planet or globe.

equator—The imaginary circle around the middle of the earth halfway between the North and South Poles.

fray—A fight.

galaxies—Very large groupings of stars, usually containing billions of stars.

galleon—A large Spanish sailing ship with three or more decks at the stern.

grapple—To hold ships together with iron hooks tied to ropes.

lance—A long wooden stick with a sharp metal spearhead.

page—A boy training for knighthood.

scurvy—A disease caused by a lack of vitamin C and characterized by spongy gums, weakness, swelling and sores.

squire—A young man who serves as a helper to knights or kings.

INDEX

Africa, 20, 22, 25, 31, 33, 36
America, 14, 18
Atlantic Ocean, 22, 40
Australia, 26

Barbosa, Diogo, 28, 33
Barbosa, Duarte, 28, 39
Brazil, 33, 34

Cabral, Captain Pedro, 20
Canary Islands, 33
Cape of Good Hope, 22, 36
Cartagena, Captain, 33–37
Cebu, 41, 43
Ceylon, 8
Charles, King, 28, 30, 37, 41
China, 18, 20, 22
Christians, 41, 43
Columbus, Christopher, 18, 20
Concepcion, 31, 36, 37, 39
Cook, Captain James, 46

da Gama, Vasco, 20, 22
de Balboa, Vasco Nunez, 34
del Cano, Juan Sebastian, 39, 43
de Lloriaga, Juan, 36

Guam, 40, 41

Ibrahim, 22–25
India, 8, 18–22, 25
Indian Ocean, 25
Indians, 18

John II, King, 17, 18, 20

Kilwa, 22

Leonora, Queen, 17
Limassawa, 41

Mactan, 43
Magellan, Beatriz, 28
Magellan, Diogo, 17, 18

Magellan, Isabel, 17
Magellanic Clouds, 40
Malacca, 7–10, 14, 25
Manuel (Duke), King, 18, 20, 28
Malays, 10, 11
Malaysia, 7, 14, 16, 22, 25
Mendoza, Captain, 37
Mohammed, 25
Morocco, 27

Pacific Ocean, 16, 40, 46
Persia, 22
Philippines, 26, 41, 43, 46
Ponte da Barca, 17
Portugal, 10, 14, 17, 18, 20, 22, 25–28, 31, 33

Quesada, Captain, 36, 37

Rio de la Plata, 34

Sabrosa, 17
Saint Julien, 36
Samar, 41
San Antonio, 31, 36, 37, 39
Santa Lucia, 34
Santiago, 31, 36, 37, 39
Sequeira, Captain, 8
Serrano, Francisco, 7–14, 18, 25, 36, 43
Serrano, John, 36, 39
Sousa, Captain, 8–14
South Sea, 34, 36, 39, 40, 46
Spain, 14, 16, 18, 28, 29, 31, 33, 39, 43
Spice Islands, 14, 16, 22, 25–30, 40–43
Strait of All Saints, 39
Strait of Magellan, 39

Trinidad, 31, 36, 37

Victoria, 31, 36, 37, 39, 43